BOULDER CITY LIBRARY

3 1432 00152 5284

D0941971

SLOW COOKER DESSERTS

T, EASY AND DELICIOUS CUSTARDS, COBBLERS, SOUFFLES, PIES, CAKES AND MORE

Jonnie Downing

Boulder City Library
701 Adams Boulevard
Boulder City, NV 89005
DEC 1   2013

DISCARD

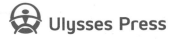
Ulysses Press

Thanks to all the slow cooker warriors out there
paving the way online and offline.

Text Copyright © 2013 by Jonnie Downing. Photographs Copyright © 2013 JudiSwinksPhotography. com except as noted below. Copyright concept and design © 2012 by Ulysses Press and its licensors. All Rights Reserved. Any unauthorized duplication in whole or in part or dissemination of this edition by any means (including but not limited to photocopying, electronic bulletin boards, and the Internet) will be prosecuted to the fullest extent of the law.

Published by:
Ulysses Press
P.O. Box 3440
Berkeley, CA 94703
www.ulyssespress.com

ISBN: 978-1-61243-124-6
Library of Congress Catalog Number 2012951894

Printed in the United States by Bang Printing

10 9 8 7 6 5 4 3 2 1

Acquisitions editor: Keith Riegert
Project editor: Alice Riegert
Managing editor: Claire Chun
Editor: Phyllis Elving
Proofreader: Elyce Berrigan-Dunlop
Cover design and layout: what!design @ whatweb.com
Cover photographs: © JudiSwinksPhotography.com
Photographs of featured recipes: © JudiSwinksPhotography.com
Clip art: all from shutterstock.com p. 8 chocolate curls © Tobik; p. 10 vanilla © Diana Taliun; p. 14 eggs © Elena Schweitzer; p. 23 peanut butter © bonchan; p. 24 lemons © Volodymyr Krasyuk; p. 26 walnuts © Standret; p. 32 pineapple © Viktar Malyshchyts; p. 34 cherries © Nattika; p. 39 plums © Viktar Malyshchyts; p. 40 apples © Maks Narodenko; p. 42 bananas © Kletr; p. 49 eggs and whisk © Africa Studio; p. 53 pumpkin © JIANG HONGYAN; p. 54 raspberries © Mauro Rodrigues; p. 58 coconut © Tomukas; p. 63 yams © Viktar Malyshchyts; p. 72 lemon zest © zkruger; p. 77 chocolate and butterscotch chips © Jenn Huls; p. 78 strawerries © Alexander Dashewsky; p. 83 cranberries and apple © Valentin Mosichev; p. 87 peaches © Maks Narodenko; p. 95 chocolate chips © M. Unal Ozmen; p. 104 blueberries © Zigzag Mountain Art; p. 109 pecans © draconus
Production: Jake Flaherty
Food stylist for featured recipes: Anna Hartman-Kenzler

IMPORTANT NOTE TO READERS: This book is independently authored and published and no sponsorship or endorsement of this book by, and no affiliation with, any trademarked brand of slow cookers or other products mentioned or pictured within is claimed or suggested. All trademarks that appear in ingredient lists, photographs, and elsewhere in this book belong to their respective owners and are used here for informational purposes only. The authors and publishers encourage readers to patronize the quality brands of slow cookers and other products mentioned and pictured in this book.

TABLE OF CONTENTS

INTRODUCTION

We all have busy lives. Between working, taking care of our families, or simply taking care of ourselves by making sure we put balanced meals on the table, it's hard to plan a dessert that is easy to make, requires little cleanup, and can complement more than one meal. That's where the slow cooker comes in.

Here I've compiled dozens of delicious slow cooker dessert recipes, many from my blog *Crockpot Ninja* (CrockpotNinja.com), that will satisfy the sweet tooth and be a hit with families, coworkers, and neighbors. Most of the recipes make several servings and keep very well in the refrigerator, so one dessert can last for several days—eliminating the need to rush out for a pint of ice cream, a frozen pie, or some other store-bought confection.

This book includes slow cooker recipes for fruit desserts, puddings, brownies, cakes, and cobblers. Whatever your hankering, there's a recipe here to satisfy and delight. All of the recipes have been tested, tasted, and approved—and are easy to make in your slow cooker. Desserts generally taste best and make the most attractive presentation when fresh ingredients are used. Sometimes, however, time is limited, so I've offered alternatives where possible. There is an "Emergency Desserts" chapter for when you need to just throw something in the slow cooker and go. No matter which chapter you open, you'll find elegant desserts that you can prepare for any occasion.

Equipment

Slow cookers come in different sizes and shapes. You can find them from 4-quart to 8-quart capacity, either round or oval. All of the recipes in this book were tested in a 6-quart round slow cooker. Some recipes call for a smaller slow cooker, which is indicated in that particular recipe. While all can be made in the 6-quart, a smaller size works better in these instances.

Many of the desserts go right into the slow cooker. For others, you'll need a few additional pieces of equipment. It's helpful to have the following on hand.

SPRINGFORM PAN One of these pans with the removable sides is essential for cheesecake recipes. Make sure you get one that will fit inside your slow cooker. For a 6-quart slow cooker, a 7-inch springform pan fits perfectly.

CORNINGWARE OR OTHER BAKING DISH Sometimes recipes call for these when a cake or pudding requires a water bath in order to remain moist. A 5–7 inch dish should fit in the 6-quart slow cooker.

TRIVET A springform pan or baking dish sometimes needs to be elevated above the bottom of the slow cooker. A good heatproof trivet or wire rack should do the trick. If necessary, a ring of aluminum foil will also work to keep the pan off the bottom of your slow cooker.

RAMEKINS For individual dessert servings, you can't beat ramekins. Four standard 3-inch ramekins will fit into a 6-quart slow cooker.

BREAD PAN To make delicious slow cooker breads, a disposable 3¾ x 8-inch bread pans in a 6-quart slow cooker works great.

When you remove your dessert from the slow cooker, be very careful. Sometimes you can turn the slow cooker upside down to flip your dessert onto a serving plate. Other times you have to remove bread pans, baking pans, or ramekins. It is not a bad idea to line the slow cooker in foil beforehand, so that you can grab onto the foil to help lift out the dessert.

Or, using oven mitts, lift the ceramic liner of your slow cooker out and place it on a heatproof surface. Unless the recipe states otherwise, allow your dessert to cool for at least 30 minutes inside the ceramic liner with the lid on.

> The better the ingredients, the better your desserts. Invest in great quality vanilla extract and spices for better flavor. I recommend Baldwin's for vanilla and Penzey's Spices for fresh flavoring.

A Word about Cooking Times

While cooking times will be similar for most slow cookers, it's good to check in on recipes from time to time to make sure your desserts aren't being overcooked.

CHAPTER 1

CAKES AND CHEESECAKES

CLASSIC CHOCOLATE CAKE

This makes a moist, crowd-pleasing chocolate cake that tastes like you brought it straight from Grandma's house.

Yield: 8 servings   *Prep time:* 20 minutes   *Cooking time:* 6 hours

Cake
¾ cup granulated sugar
¾ cup unbleached all-purpose flour
½ teaspoon baking soda
¼ teaspoon salt
⅓ cup unsweetened cocoa powder
¼ cup canola oil
½ cup buttermilk
½ teaspoon vanilla extract
1 large egg

Frosting
½ cup (1 stick) unsalted butter, softened
2⅔ cups sifted powdered sugar
½ cup sifted unsweetened cocoa powder
⅓ cup heavy cream, plus more if needed
1½ teaspoons vanilla extract

Grease an 8-inch round cake pan with shortening or butter, or coat it with cooking spray. In a mixing bowl, blend all the cake ingredients until they are mixed very well, and then mix by hand or with an electric mixer until smooth, about 3 minutes.

Pour the batter into the prepared pan and place in your slow cooker. Cover the top of the pan with several paper towels, careful not to touch the batter. Cover the slow cooker, venting the lid slightly with a toothpick or spatula handle to allow steam to escape. Cook on low for 6 hours, until a toothpick inserted near the center comes out clean.

Let cool, in the slow cooker with the lid removed. Then gently and carefully lift the cake pan out of the slow cooker. Run a knife around the inside edge and invert the pan to turn the cake onto a serving platter.

MAKE THE FROSTING: Using a stand mixer with the whip attachment, whip up the butter until it has a creamy texture and is off-white in color. In a separate bowl, mix the powdered sugar with the cocoa. With the mixer going, blend in the cocoa-sugar mixture alternately with the cream and vanilla so the texture stays smooth and creamy. If the mixture seems a little dry, carefully add a bit more cream. Continue beating until you have that fluffy frosting that you want.

Frost the cake and serve.

YELLOW CAKE WITH MILK CHOCOLATE FROSTING

This classic yellow cake is wonderful with the milk chocolate frosting we've paired it with, but you can serve it with any kind of frosting you want, or none at all. It's that good.

Yield: 8 servings   *Prep time:* 20 minutes   *Cooking time:* 6 hours

Cake

¾ cup granulated sugar

¼ cup plus 1 tablespoon shortening

1¼ cups unbleached all-purpose flour

½ teaspoon salt

1½ teaspoons baking powder

⅔ cup reduced-fat (2%) milk

1 large egg

1 large egg yolk

1 teaspoon vanilla extract

Frosting

1 ounce milk chocolate

1 cup granulated sugar

1 tablespoon light corn syrup

⅔ cup half and half

⅛ teaspoon salt

1 tablespoon unsalted butter

½ teaspoon vanilla extract

Coat an 8-inch round cake pan with cooking spray.

In a mixing bowl, using an electric mixer, combine the sugar, shortening, flour, salt, baking powder, and milk. Add the egg, egg yolk, and vanilla and beat until smooth.

Pour the batter into the prepared cake pan. Set a trivet in the slow cooker and place the pan on the trivet. Cover and cook on low for 6 hours. Let cool in the slow cooker, uncovered, then lift the cake pan out of the slow cooker.

While the cake is cooling, make the frosting: Combine all the ingredients except the butter and vanilla in a small saucepan. Cook over medium heat stirring constantly until the chocolate is melted and the frosting has reached the soft ball stage (a bit of frosting dropped into very cold water will form a soft ball). Remove from the heat and stir in the butter. Let cool. When it has almost reached room temperature, add the vanilla and beat with an electric mixer until the frosting is thickened.

Invert cake onto a plate and when completely cooled, ice the cake with the frosting.

INDIVIDUAL PLUM BUCKLE CAKES

These individual plum buckle cakes are great topped with a scoop of vanilla ice cream. Serve them right in the ramekins—you'll need four of them—for a dessert that's sure to be remembered.

Yield: 4 servings   *Prep time:* 15 minutes   *Cooking time:* 4 hours

½ cup (1 stick) unsalted butter, softened

½ cup plus 1 tablespoon granulated sugar, divided

1 large egg

¾ cup unbleached all-purpose flour

½ teaspoon baking powder

⅛ teaspoon salt

⅛ teaspoon ground nutmeg

⅙ cup reduced-fat (2%) milk (fill a ⅓ cup measure halfway)

2 cups sliced unpeeled ripe plums

½ teaspoon ground cinnamon

Using a stand mixer or an electric hand mixer, cream the butter and ½ cup sugar until well blended. Add the egg, beating the mixture thoroughly.

In a separate bowl, mix the flour, baking powder, salt, and nutmeg until well blended. Stir half of this dry mixture into the butter mixture and add the milk, stirring to fully combine but not until smooth. Add the rest of the dry ingredient mixture and blend until all ingredients are fully combined, but not smooth.

Coat the insides of 4 individual ramekins with cooking spray. Pour in the batter and arrange plum slices in a circular pattern in each ramekin. In a small bowl, mix together the remaining 1 tablespoon sugar and the cinnamon. Sprinkle over the batter in the ramekins.

Place the ramekins in the slow cooker. Cover and cook on low for 4 to 5 hours, or until a wooden toothpick inserted near the center comes out clean. Serve warm with vanilla ice cream. Yum!

CHOCOLATE LAVA CAKE

This is an amped-up and shrunken-down chocolate cake, gooey and delicious. It's perfect for a small dinner party, or a family dinner that you want to make a little bit special. Serve in individual ramekins along with whipped topping and fresh fruit, if you desire.

Yield: 4 servings   *Prep time:* 20 minutes   *Cooking time:* 4 hours

4 ounces bittersweet baking bar, chopped into ½-inch pieces, divided

3 tablespoons heavy cream

⅓ cup unsalted butter

3 tablespoons unbleached all-purpose flour

1 large whole egg

2 large egg yolks

¼ teaspoon vanilla extract

3 tablespoons granulated sugar

Using a double boiler or a heatproof bowl over simmering, not boiling, water, melt 1½ ounces chocolate and combine with the cream. Whisk the mixture gently until blended. Refrigerate for about 2 hours. Once it's firm, form 4 balls out of it.

Spray 4 ramekins with nonstick cooking spray. Start making the cakes. Melt the remaining 2½ ounces chocolate in a double boiler (like above) with the butter.

Using an electric mixer, whisk the flour, eggs, egg yolks, vanilla and sugar on high for about 5 minutes, until the mixture is nice and creamy. Fold the chocolate-butter mixture into the egg-vanilla mixture until it's just combined—not mixing too much. Put the cake batter into the ramekins and drop 1 of your refrigerated balls of chocolate in the center.

Line your slow cooker with foil and place the ramekins down inside. Pour hot water around them until the water comes halfway up the side. Cover the slow cooker and cook on low for 4 hours, until the cake is done. You'll be able to tell if a toothpick, inserted into the cake BESIDE the place where you put the chocolate ball, comes out clean. Keep in mind that the cakes do have a gooey center, so if the toothpick trick doesn't work, press

down lightly on the spongy rim of the cake. If it bounces back at your touch, odds are it is ready.

Lift the ramekins out of the slow cooker by gripping the ends of the aluminum foil and let cool a few minutes before inverting onto a plate. Serve warm.

POUND CAKE

Pound cake is delicious served with ice cream, whipped cream, fresh fruit, fruit compote, or all of them. This simple pound cake is so easy to make in the slow cooker! It may not look like a traditional pound cake, but it sure tastes like it.

Yield: 12 servings   *Prep time:* 10 minutes   *Cooking time:* 7 to 8 hours

3 large eggs

1 cup (2 sticks) unsalted butter, softened

1 cup sour cream

1 teaspoon vanilla extract

½ teaspoon baking soda

½ teaspoon salt

2 cups granulated sugar

2½ cups unbleached all-purpose flour

1 teaspoon grated orange peel

Grease the inside of your slow cooker with shortening or butter or coat with cooking spray. I prefer shortening for pound cake because it provides a little more substance in the coating than butter or cooking spray.

Using an electric mixer, blend all the ingredients until creamy and thick. Pour the batter into the slow cooker. Cover and cook on low for 7 to 8 hours, until a toothpick inserted near the center comes out clean. Let cool completely, uncovered, and flip the slow cooker upside down to transfer the cake onto a serving plate.

SUPER-SIMPLE SLOW COOKER CHEESECAKE

A cheesecake can be labor intensive, and this one tastes like it took forever—but it actually requires very little effort on your part. What could be better than that? You'll need a springform pan and a trivet.

Yield: 10 servings   *Prep time:* 15 minutes   *Cooking time:* 3 hours

3 tablespoons unsalted butter, melted

¼ cup finely chopped pecans

2 tablespoons light brown sugar

1 cup graham cracker crumbs

2 (8-ounce) packages cream cheese

¾ cup granulated sugar

2 large eggs, at room temperature

¼ cup heavy cream

1 tablespoon unbleached all-purpose flour

1 teaspoon vanilla extract

To make the crust, mix the first 4 ingredients together in a bowl. Press into the bottom of a 6-inch springform pan. You'll need to be using a larger slow cooker for this recipe.

Using an electric mixer, beat the cream cheese until fluffy. Beat in the granulated sugar and then the eggs, one at a time. Add the cream, flour, and vanilla, beating to make a smooth batter. Pour into the crust in the springform pan.

Place a trivet in the bottom of your slow cooker and set the springform pan on the trivet. Cook, covered, for 2½ to 3 hours. Turn off the slow cooker and leave the cheesecake in the slow cooker (covered) for 1 to 2 hours, or until cool. Remove from the slow cooker and refrigerate, covered, for at least an hour before serving. Then run a thin knife or metal spatula around the inner edge of the pan and gently detach the rim.

N'AWLINS PRALINE CHEESECAKE

The best pralines I've ever had came from New Orleans, on a trip to take my daughter to see Tulane University. She still dreams of getting her doctorate there. I still dream of the pralines. This cheesecake reminds me of that special trip, and it tastes out of this world. The pecans and brown sugar in the crust combine with the creaminess of the cheesecake to create that special praline taste.

Yield: 8 to 10 servings   *Prep time:* 40 minutes   *Cooking time:* 2 to 3 hours

Cheesecake

1 cup graham cracker crumbs

¾ cup plus 2 tablespoons packed light brown sugar, divided

¼ cup finely chopped pecans

3 tablespoons unsalted butter, melted

2 (8-ounce) packages cream cheese, at room temperature

2 large eggs

¼ cup heavy cream

1 tablespoon unbleached all-purpose flour

1 teaspoon vanilla extract

Pralines

1½ cups toasted pecans

1½ white sugar

¾ cup brown sugar

¼ cup plus 2 tablespoons butter

½ cup whole milk

1 teaspoon vanilla extract

In a bowl, combine the graham cracker crumbs, 2 tablespoons brown sugar, and chopped pecans. Pour the melted butter over the crumb mixture and stir to combine. Press into the bottom of a 7-inch springform pan.

Using an electric mixer, beat the cream cheese with the remaining ¾ cup brown sugar until light and creamy. Beat in the eggs, cream, flour, and vanilla. Pour the cheesecake filling over the prepared crust in the springform pan.

Place a trivet in your slow cooker and set the cheesecake on the trivet. Cover and cook on low for 2 to 3 hours. Turn off the slow cooker and leave the cheesecake in the slow cooker, covered, for 1 to 2 hours, or until cool.

While the cheesecake is cooking, prepare the pralines: Line a baking sheet with aluminum foil. Put the pecans, sugars, butter, milk, and vanilla into a medium saucepan and heat until it reaches soft ball stage (when a small bit of the mixture, dropped into cold water, forms a soft ball you can flatten with your fingertips).

Using a teaspoon, drop large dollops of the mixture onto the lined baking sheet. Let cool completely.

Remove the cheesecake from the slow cooker and refrigerate, covered, for at least an hour before serving. Then run a thin knife or metal spatula around the inner edge of the pan and gently detach the rim. Top the cheesecake with the crushed pralines.

ORANGE CHEESECAKE

Remember Creamsicles? This lovely cheesecake will take you back to your youth, and memories of that yummy orange treat. Serve this to your family or take it to an event and become the envy of all those who'd never dream of trying to make a cheesecake, let alone one that tastes like this!

Yield: 7 servings   *Prep time:* 30 minutes   *Cooking time:* 2½ to 3 hours

¾ cup graham cracker crumbs

3 tablespoons unsalted butter, melted

⅔ cup plus 2 tablespoons granulated sugar, divided

2 (8-ounce) packages cream cheese, softened

2 large eggs plus 1 large egg yolk

¼ cup orange juice concentrate, thawed

1 teaspoon grated orange peel

1 tablespoon unbleached all-purpose flour

½ teaspoon vanilla extract

To make the crust, combine the graham cracker crumbs, butter, and 2 tablespoons sugar in a small mixing bowl. Press into the bottom of a 7-inch springform pan.

Using an electric mixer, combine the cream cheese and remaining ⅔ cup sugar. Add the eggs and yolk, one a time, beating well after each addition. Add the orange juice, orange peel, flour, and vanilla. Beat for about 2 minutes, until smooth and creamy. Pour the batter over the crust in the springform pan.

Place a trivet in the bottom of your slow cooker and set the cheesecake on the trivet. Cover and cook on high for 2½ to 3 hours. Turn off the heat and let cool, covered, for 1 to 2 hours, until the cheesecake is cool enough to remove. Refrigerate, covered, for at least an hour before serving. Then run a thin knife or metal spatula around the inner edge of the pan and gently detach the rim.

GERMAN CHOCOLATE CAKE

Named after a man named Sam German, the German chocolate cake is a family favorite—as long as the family likes coconut!

Yield: 8 servings   *Prep time:* 20 minutes   *Cooking time:* 6 hours

Cake

2 ounces German's sweet chocolate

¼ cup hot water

½ cup (1 stick) unsalted butter, softened

1 cup granulated sugar

2 large eggs

1⅛ cups unbleached all-purpose flour

½ teaspoon baking soda

⅛ teaspoon salt

½ cup buttermilk

½ teaspoon vanilla extract

Topping

1 cup sweetened condensed milk

1 cup granulated sugar

3 large egg yolks beaten with 1 teaspoon water

½ cup (1 stick) salted butter, softened

1 teaspoon vanilla extract

1 cup sweetened flaked coconut

In a small saucepan over medium heat, melt the chocolate in the water.

With an electric mixer, cream the butter with the sugar in a mixing bowl; add the eggs, mixing well. Add the melted chocolate. Set your mixer to slow and add some flour, baking soda, and salt, then a bit of the buttermilk, then more flour mixture, until you finally end on the flour mixture. Add the vanilla and mix thoroughly.

Coat the inside of your slow cooker with cooking spray. Pour in the batter and cover, venting the lid with a toothpick. Cook on low for 6 hours, or until a toothpick inserted near the center comes out clean.

While the cake is cooling, make the topping: In a medium saucepan over low heat, stir together the condensed milk, sugar, egg yolks, butter, and vanilla. Heat, stirring the entire time, until the butter is melted and the mixture thickens. Once it has the desired consistency, remove it from the heat and gently stir in the coconut until completely blended.

Invert the cake onto a serving plate. Spread the warm topping liberally over your cooled cake.

CHOCOLATE SWIRL CHEESECAKE WITH PEANUT BUTTER

Who doesn't like the combination of peanut butter and chocolate? This cheesecake fills the bill to satisfy that sweet craving. You'll be the cooking star!

Yield: 7 to 10 servings   *Prep time:* 20 minutes   *Cooking time:* 2 to 2½ hours

1 cup graham cracker crumbs

3 tablespoons unsalted butter, melted

2 tablespoons plus ⅔ cup packed light brown sugar, divided

1½ (8-ounce) packages cream cheese, at room temperature

2 large eggs

1 tablespoon unbleached all-purpose flour

⅓ cup creamy peanut butter

½ teaspoon vanilla extract

½ cup chocolate chips, melted

In a bowl, mix together the graham cracker crumbs, butter, and 2 tablespoons brown sugar. Press into the bottom of a 7-inch springform pan, patting down the mixture to make a smooth crust.

Using an electric mixer, mix the cream cheese and remaining ⅔ cup brown sugar. Add the eggs and beat for about 2 minutes, until thoroughly combined. Add the flour, peanut butter, and vanilla and beat for 2 more minutes. Reserve ½ cup of the batter and pour the rest over the crust in the springform pan.

Combine the melted chocolate chips and the reserved ½ cup of batter in a small mixing bowl. Pour the mixture over the batter in the pan. Use a knife to make swirl patterns on the top, without digging into the crust.

Place a trivet in the bottom of your slow cooker and set the cheesecake on the trivet. Cover and cook on low for 2 to 2½ hours. Turn off the heat and leave the pan in the slow cooker with the lid on for another 1 to 2 hours to cool. Remove from the slow cooker and refrigerate for at least an hour to serve chilled; then run a thin knife or metal spatula around the inner edge of the pan and gently detach the rim.

LUSCIOUS LEMON CAKE

Light and lemony, this cake has a soft and velvety texture that works especially well for those nights when a heavy dessert just won't do.

Yield: 5 to 7 servings   *Prep time:* 15 minutes   *Cooking time:* 2 to 3 hours

3 large eggs, separated
¼ cup lemon juice
1 teaspoon grated lemon peel
3 tablespoons unsalted butter, softened
1½ cups skim milk
¾ cup granulated sugar
¼ teaspoon salt
¼ cup unbleached all-purpose flour

Using an electric mixer, beat the eggs whites until stiff peaks form. In a separate bowl, mix the egg yolks with the lemon juice, peel, butter, and milk. Add the sugar and salt and beat until smooth. Fold in the egg whites.

Spray the slow cooker with nonstick cooking spray. Spoon the batter into the slow cooker. Cover and cook on high for 2 to 3 hours. Serve directly from the slow cooker onto dessert plates.

CARROT CAKE WITH CREAM CHEESE ICING

A classic carrot cake is an appropriate dessert for any meal, any function, any time!

Yield: 10 servings   *Prep time:* 20 minutes   *Cooking time:* 3 hours

Cake

2 large eggs

1 cup granulated sugar

1 cup packed light brown sugar

⅔ cup canola oil

1½ cups unbleached all-purpose flour

1 teaspoon baking soda

1 teaspoon salt

1 tablespoon ground cinnamon

1 cup chopped walnuts

1½ cups finely shredded carrots

Cream Cheese Icing

4 cups powdered sugar

1 (8-ounce) package cream cheese, softened (I use the reduced-fat kind)

1 teaspoon vanilla extract

2 to 3 tablespoons half and half

Using an electric mixer, beat together the eggs, sugars, and canola oil. Stir in the flour, baking soda, salt, and cinnamon, mixing well. Gently stir in the walnuts and carrots.

    With butter or shortening, grease a cake pan that fits into your slow cooker (for a 6-quart slow cooker, an 8-inch round cake pan should fit). Transfer the batter to the prepared pan. Place a trivet in the slow cooker and set the cake pan on the trivet.

    Cover and cook on high for 3 hours, or until a toothpick inserted near the center comes out clean. Cool in the slow cooker, uncovered.

    While the cake is cooling, make the frosting: Using a stand mixer (or vigorously using a hand beater), cream together the powdered sugar and cream cheese until smooth. Beat in the vanilla and then the half and half, a little at a time, until you have the desired thick and creamy consistency.

Once the cake has completely cooled, invert onto a serving plate, running a knife along the sides to dislodge and frost.

WALNUT APPLE COFFEE CAKE

This cake is brimming with lovely spices to fill your home while it is cooking. Invite the neighbors over for some warm cake and coffee, and you'll be the neighborhood favorite.

Yield: 6 servings   *Prep time:* 15 minutes   *Cooking time:* 3½ to 4 hours

2 large eggs

1 cup canola oil

2 cups granulated sugar

2 teaspoons vanilla extract

2 cups unbleached all-purpose flour

1 teaspoon baking soda

1 teaspoon ground nutmeg

1 teaspoon ground cinnamon

½ teaspoon ground cloves

2 cups peeled and finely chopped Granny Smith or other tart apples

1 cup chopped English walnuts (optional)

Beat together the eggs, oil, sugar, and vanilla. Add the flour, baking soda, and spices, mixing well. Fold in the apples and walnuts.

Use cooking spray to coat the inside of a dish that fits into your slow cooker. Pour in the batter. Place the dish in the slow cooker.

Carefully pour hot water into the cooker around the cake so that it comes about ⅔ up the side of the dish. Cover, but tilt the lid a bit to allow steam to escape. Cook on low for 3½ to 4 hours. Cool in the slow cooker, covered, for about 30 minutes before removing the baking dish. Slide a knife around the edge and invert onto a plate.

CHAPTER 2

COBBLERS, CRISPS, AND OTHER FRUIT DESSERTS

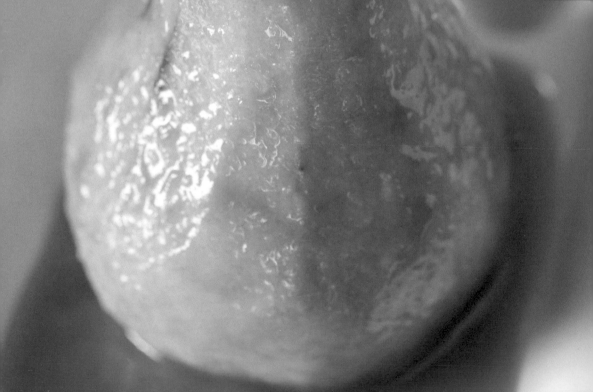

PEACH COBBLER

Nothing says comfort food like a nice, warm cobbler. Peaches are just the right fruit to use, though you can substitute blueberries or pitted cherries or plums if you're so inclined.

Yield: 6 servings   *Prep time:* 20 minutes   *Cooking time:* 7 hours

1 cup unbleached all-purpose flour

1¼ cups granulated sugar, divided

½ cup (1 stick) unsalted butter, softened

1 teaspoon baking powder

⅛ teaspoon salt

1 teaspoon vanilla extract

½ cup reduced-fat (2%) milk

2 pounds fresh peaches, peeled and sliced (about 2 cups)

½ teaspoon ground cinnamon

½ cup hot water

In a bowl, combine the flour, 1 cup sugar, butter, baking powder, salt, vanilla, and milk. Mix thoroughly to make a smooth batter.

Coat the inside of the slow cooker with cooking spray. Spread the peaches over the bottom of the slow cooker, sprinkle with the cinnamon, and cover with the batter. Cover and cook on high for 1 hour.

In a small bowl, stir together the remaining ¼ cup sugar and the water; pour over the cobbler. Cover again and cook on low for another 6 hours.

MINI BERRY COBBLERS

These mini cobblers are perfect when you're serving dinner for four. Other fruits can be substituted for the berries—just make sure to cut the fruit into small pieces so it will fit nicely into the ramekins.

Yield: 4 servings   *Prep time:* 20 minutes   *Cooking time:* 4 hours

1 cup unbleached all-purpose flour

1 ¼ cups granulated sugar, divided

½ cup (1 stick) unsalted butter, softened

1 teaspoon baking powder

⅛ teaspoon salt

1 teaspoon vanilla

½ cup reduced-fat (2%) milk

2 cups fresh berries (I prefer blackberries and raspberries)

½ teaspoon ground cinnamon

½ cup hot water

In a bowl, combine the flour, 1 cup sugar, butter, baking powder, salt, vanilla, and milk. Mix thoroughly to make a smooth batter.

Coat the insides of 4 (3-inch) ramekins with cooking spray. Divide the berries among the ramekins, sprinkle them with the cinnamon, and cover with the batter. Place a trivet in your slow cooker and set the ramekins on the trivet. Cover and cook on high for 1 hour.

In a small bowl, stir together the remaining ¼ cup sugar and the water; pour over the cobblers. Cover again and cook on low for another 3 hours.

PINEAPPLE CRISP

Cracker crumbs are the secret to the delightful texture of this warm pineapple dessert.

Yield: 4 servings   *Prep time:* 5 minutes   *Cooking time:* 2 hours

2 (20-ounce) cans chunk pineapple, drained or 2½ cups
    chunked fresh pineapple

¾ cup finely ground Ritz or similar crackers

1 cup packed light brown sugar

¼ cup (½ stick) unsalted butter, divided

Pour half of the pineapple into a 4½-quart slow cooker. Cover with half the cracker crumbs and half the brown sugar; dot with half the butter. Cover with the rest of the pineapple, then the remaining cracker crumbs, brown sugar, and butter.

Cover the slow cooker and cook on low for 2 hours. Serve warm.

FRUIT CRISP

A wonderful dessert for a crisp fall day—apples, pears, and sweet spices. It just makes you think of autumn.

Yield: 10 servings   *Prep time:* 5 minutes   *Cooking time:* 6 to 7 hours

6 cups peeled and sliced pears

1 cup dried cherries

6 cups peeled and sliced Golden Delicious apples

1 teaspoon grated orange peel

½ cup granulated sugar

3 teaspoons ground cinnamon, divided

1 cup rolled oats

1 cup unbleached all-purpose flour

¾ cup packed light brown sugar

¼ teaspoon ground mace

½ teaspoon grated fresh ginger

¾ cup (1 ½ sticks) unsalted butter, softened

Coat the inside of your slow cooker with cooking spray.

In a large bowl, stir together the pears, cherries, apples, orange peel, granulated sugar, and 1 teaspoon cinnamon. Mix thoroughly.

In another bowl, combine the oats, flour, brown sugar, mace, ginger, and remaining 2 teaspoons cinnamon. Mix together with the fruit and pour into the slow cooker. Dot with the butter.

Cover and cook on low for 6 to 7 hours, or until the fruit is fully cooked. Serve warm.

CHERRY CRISP

Bursting with fresh cherry flavor, this makes a satisfying ending to any meal. Top it with vanilla ice cream, if you wish.

Yield: 8 servings   *Prep time:* 40 minutes   *Cooking time:* 5 hours

½ cup quick-cooking rolled oats
⅔ cup packed light brown sugar
1 cup plus 1 teaspoon granulated sugar, divided
½ cup unbleached all-purpose flour
⅓ cup unsalted butter, softened
2 pounds fresh cherries, pitted
1 cup water

Coat the inside of your slow cooker with cooking spray. In a bowl, mix together the oats, brown sugar, 1 teaspoon granulated sugar, and flour. Cut in the butter to make crumbles.

In a large saucepan over medium heat, bring the cherries to a simmer with the water and remaining 1 cup granulated sugar for about 20 minutes, until the cherries are soft. Pour into the slow cooker. Cover with the crumb mixture.

Cover and cook on low for 5 hours. Serve out of the slow cooker onto individual plates.

APPLE BROWN BETTY

This classic dessert is so easy—and so good—that you might find yourself making it several times a month. As for most of my apple recipes, I prefer Granny Smith apples. They hold their shape better than any other kind of apple, and their natural tartness keeps a dish from being overly sweet.

Yield: 4 servings   *Prep time:* 25 minutes   *Cooking time:* 5 to 7 hours

3 pounds Granny Smith apples, peeled, cored, and chunked

10 slices of bread, cubed

¾ cup packed light brown sugar

¾ teaspoon ground cinnamon

¼ teaspoon ground nutmeg

dash of salt

½ cup (1 stick) unsalted butter, melted

Place the chunked apples in your slow cooker.

In a bowl, combine the bread cubes, brown sugar, cinnamon, nutmeg, and salt. Toss with the melted butter. Cover the apples with the bread mixture. Cover and cook on low for 5 to 7 hours. Serve warm or at room temperature.

PEARS WITH CARAMEL AND MAPLE

This dish is full of the tastes of autumn. Enjoy it with ice cream or whipped cream for a fancy flourish.

Yield: 6 servings   *Prep time:* 5 minutes   *Cooking time:* 2½ to 3 hours

6 Bosc pears with stems attached, peeled, cored from the
   bottom
½ cup pure maple syrup
1 cup caramel sauce
grated peel from 1 lemon

Coat the inside of your slow cooker with cooking spray. Set the pears in the slow cooker, stems up.

In a bowl, stir together the maple syrup, caramel sauce, and lemon peel. Pour over the pears in the slow cooker. Cover and cook on high for 2½ to 3 hours. Transfer the pears to individual serving dishes and spoon the sauce over them.

BLUEBERRY CREAM CHEESE COBBLER

This rich-tasting cobbler has been lightened up through the use of reduced-fat cream cheese and nonfat milk.

Yield: 12 servings   *Prep time:* 15 minutes   *Cooking time:* 6 hours

1 loaf fresh Italian bread, cut into cubes (about 4 cups)

1 pint fresh blueberries

1 (8-ounce) package reduced-fat cream cheese, cut into cubes

1½ cups nonfat milk

6 large eggs

Butter the inside of your slow cooker or coat with cooking spray. Layer half the bread cubes and half the blueberries in the slow cooker, then add half the cream cheese cubes. Repeat the layers with the remaining bread, blueberries, and cream cheese.

In a bowl, whisk together the milk and eggs. Pour over the layers in the slow cooker; it will saturate the bread.

Cover and cook on low for 6 hours, or until a tester inserted near the center comes out clean. Serve warm.

PLUM CRUMBLE

Serving this crumb-topped plum dessert in individual ramekins adds a special touch.

Yield: 4 servings   *Prep time:* 30 minutes   *Cooking time:* 2 hours

1 pound fresh unpeeled plums, pitted and quartered
1 cup rolled oats
1 cup packed light brown sugar
1 teaspoon ground cinnamon
½ teaspoon ground cloves
½ cup (1 stick) unsalted butter, softened slightly

In a medium saucepan over medium heat, simmer the plums with a small amount of water for about 15 minutes, until softened. Meanwhile, combine all the other ingredients together in a bowl to form a crumbly mixture.

Portion the cooked plums into 4 individual ramekins and top with the crumble mixture. Set the ramekins in the slow cooker. Cover and cook on low for 2 hours. Serve warm.

GINGER APPLE DESSERT

A touch of ginger turns this apple dessert into something a little different.

Yield: 10 servings   *Prep time:* 10 minutes   *Cooking time:* 5 to 6 hours

5 Granny Smith apples, peeled, cored, and sliced

½ cup packed light brown sugar

½ cup unbleached all-purpose flour

¾ cup rolled oats

½ teaspoon ground nutmeg

½ teaspoon grated or minced fresh ginger (or 1 teaspoon ground ginger)

½ teaspoon ground cinnamon

½ to ⅔ stick unsalted butter, softened

Grease the inside of your slow cooker. Place the apple slices in the slow cooker.

Combine all the remaining ingredients in a bowl, cutting in the butter with a pastry blender to make a crumbly mixture. Sprinkle the crumbles over the apples in the slow cooker.

Cover and cook on low for 5 to 6 hours. Serve warm.

CHERRY PIE WITH FRESH WHIPPED CREAM

Don't expect a flaky crust for this take on a classic cherry pie—a slow cooker simply isn't built for that. But with its delicious graham cracker crust, this pie is sure to be a winner.

Yield: 8 servings   *Prep time:* 40 minutes   *Cooking time:* 3 hours

Pie

2 pounds fresh cherries, pitted

1 cup water

1¼ cups granulated sugar, divided

1 cup graham cracker crumbs

½ teaspoon ground cinnamon

¼ cup (½ stick) unsalted butter, melted

Whipped Cream

½ cup container heavy cream

2 tablespoons sugar

In a large saucepan over medium heat, simmer the cherries in the water with 1 cup sugar for about 20 minutes, until softened.

Meanwhile, mix the graham cracker crumbs with the remaining ¼ cup sugar, cinnamon, and melted butter. Coat the slow cooker with cooking spray and press the crumb mixture into the bottom and lower edges of the slow cooker. Top with the cooked cherries and sauce. Cover and cook on low for 3 hours.

Meanwhile, make the whipped cream. Using the wire whip attachment on an electric mixer, whip the cream just until stiff peaks form, slowly adding the sugar as you beat it. Refrigerate until serving.

Once the pie has cooked, scoop into individual serving dishes and top with whipped cream.

BANANAS FOSTER

The rum, bananas, and brown sugar give this dessert such a warm and decadent feeling that you'll imagine that you're relaxing on a tropical island. Or wish you were.

Yield: 6 servings   *Prep time:* 5 minutes   *Cooking time:* 1 hour

½ cup (1 stick) unsalted butter
½ cup packed light brown sugar
6 bananas, cut into 1-inch pieces
¼ cup dark rum
vanilla ice cream
toasted sweetened flaked coconut (optional)

Melt the butter in the bottom of your slow cooker on low. Stir in the brown sugar. Stir in the banana pieces and the rum.

Cover and cook on low for 1 hour. Serve warm over vanilla ice cream. If you wish, sprinkle on some toasted coconut.

PEANUTTY ORANGE BAKED APPLES

Reminiscent of warm apple pie, but with a twist, this is one you'll make again and again. If you wish, serve the apples with whipped cream or ice cream.

Yield: 6 servings   *Prep time:* 15 minutes   *Cooking time:* 8 hours

2 tablespoons creamy peanut butter

2 tablespoons unsalted butter

6 Granny Smith or other tart apples

3 tablespoons unbleached all-purpose flour

½ cup granulated sugar

1 teaspoon grated orange peel

¾ teaspoon ground cinnamon

¼ teaspoon ground nutmeg

dash of salt

⅔ cup orange juice

⅔ cup water

¼ cup roasted peanuts

Mix the butter and peanut butter together and set aside. Core the apples and peel them about a third of the way down from the top. Fill the cavities with the peanut butter and butter mixture, cut into chunks. Set the apples in the slow cooker.

In a bowl, combine the flour, sugar, orange peel, cinnamon, nutmeg, and salt; sprinkle over the apples. Pour the orange juice and water around the apples.

Cover and cook on low for 8 hours, or until the apples are tender. Garnish with roasted peanuts and serve warm.

CHAPTER 3

CUSTARDS AND PUDDINGS

BOURBON CUSTARD WITH NUTMEG

You'll need a baking dish and a trivet for cooking this silky custard. (A 6-inch dish works in most 6-quart slow cookers.) Add a nice bottle of bourbon and you're good to go for a creamy, old-fashioned dessert.

Yield: 6 servings   *Prep time:* 20 minutes   *Cooking time:* 2½ hours

2 cups whole milk

3 large eggs, lightly beaten

⅓ cup granulated sugar

1 teaspoon vanilla extract

¼ teaspoon salt

1 tablespoon Kentucky bourbon

½ teaspoon ground nutmeg

freshly ground nutmeg for garnish (optional)

In a medium saucepan, scald the milk (bring it almost to a boil) and remove it from the heat. In a bowl, whisk together the eggs, sugar, vanilla, and salt. Slowly whisk in the scalded milk, bourbon, and finally the nutmeg.

Use cooking spray to coat the inside of a baking dish that fits into your slow cooker. Pour in the custard mixture. Place a trivet in your slow cooker and set the baking dish on the trivet. Carefully pour hot water around the dish until it comes about an inch up along the sides.

Cover and cook on high for 2½ hours, or until the custard is firm. You'll know it's done when a knife inserted near the center comes out clean. Garnish with freshly grated nutmeg, if desired. Serve warm, or let cool and then cover and refrigerate to serve cold.

INDIVIDUAL CHOCOLATE SOUFFLÉS

These little chocolate soufflés are a crowd-pleaser every time. The last time I made them, I had to use three slow cookers! Melt the chocolate carefully to avoid burning it–take it from someone who knows.

Yield: 3 servings   *Prep time:* 20 minutes   *Cooking time:* 1 hour

3 tablespoons unsalted butter
2 ounces semisweet chocolate
6 tablespoons sugar
1 tablespoon cornstarch
1 large egg
1 large egg yolk

Melt the butter and chocolate together in a small saucepan over low heat. In a bowl, mix the sugar and cornstarch. Whisk in the chocolate mixture. Add the egg and egg yolk, whisking until smooth.

Transfer the mixture into ramekins (recipe fits 3) but don't fill them all the way. Place them on a trivet in your slow cooker. Cover and cook on high for 1 hour. The middle should still be sort of jiggly.

STICKY TOFFEE PUDDING

It was a dilemma as to whether to classify this as a cake or as a pudding. It's technically a cake—a traditional British steamed cake. But the name does say "pudding," so where else would you look? This dessert is a little labor intensive, but totally worth it. You'll need a 5-inch CorningWare or other lidded baking dish to use in the slow cooker. Make the toffee sauce and custard while the cake is cooking.

Yield: 6 to 8 servings   *Prep time:* 1 hour   *Cooking time:* 3 hours

Cake
1¼ cups pitted dates, divided
¾ cup water
½ teaspoon baking soda
½ teaspoon baking powder
1¼ cups unbleached all-purpose flour
½ teaspoon salt
¾ cup packed light brown sugar
2 large eggs
1½ teaspoons vanilla extract
¼ cup (½ stick) unsalted butter, melted

Crème Anglaise
½ cup whole milk
¼ cup granulated sugar
¼ teaspoon salt
5 large egg yolks
1 teaspoon vanilla extract

Toffee Sauce
½ cup (1 stick) unsalted butter
1 cup packed light brown sugar
⅔ cup heavy cream
1 tablespoon spiced rum

Coat the inside of a 5-inch CorningWare casserole or other bakeware with cooking spray. Lightly dust with flour.

Chop half of the dates as small as you can get them and set aside. In a medium saucepan over high heat, bring the water to a boil, then add the whole dates and the baking soda. Remove from the heat and let sit for 5 minutes. Meanwhile, stir the baking powder, flour, and salt together in a bowl.

Using a food processor, grind the chopped dates and brown sugar together until the mixture has a grainy texture. Drain the whole soaked dates, setting them aside to use later, and pour the soaking liquid into the food processor with the date and brown sugar mixture. Add the eggs and vanilla and process until smooth. With the processor running, add the melted butter through the feed tube; combine thoroughly. Turn off the food processor, and then stir in the whole soaked dates.

Carefully combine the dry ingredients with the date mixture. Transfer the mixture into the prepared dish and cover with its lid or foil. Set the dish in the slow cooker.

Boil 2 cups of water and carefully pour it around the sides of the pudding dish until it reaches about halfway up. (You can discard whatever water is left, or make yourself a nice cup of tea.)

Cover the slow cooker and cook on high for 3 hours, until the cake is cooked through and has a springy feel when you touch it.

While the pudding is cooking, make the crème anglaise and toffee sauce. In a medium saucepan, heat the milk over medium heat until it steams, but don't let it boil. While the milk is heating, whisk the sugar, salt, and egg yolks in a bowl until the mixture is smooth and light yellow. Reduce the heat to low and add the egg mixture to the scaled milk, stirring constantly, for about 5 minutes, until the custard is thickened enough to leave a film on a spoon when you stir it. Stir in the vanilla. Strain the mixture through a fine-mesh strainer or cheesecloth into a serving pitcher.

Make the toffee sauce: Melt the butter in a medium saucepan over medium heat. Whisk in the brown sugar for about 4 minutes, until the sugar is melted and the mixture is smooth and slightly puffed up. Slowly add the cream and rum and then whisk quickly to combine. Immediately turn down the heat to low and simmer for about 5 to 10 minutes, stirring until the mixture is fluffy and frothy.

When the pudding has fully cooked, let cool for 15 minutes, in the slow cooker, uncovered, then turn out onto a serving plate. To serve, slice the cake onto individual serving dishes and top with crème anglaise and warm toffee sauce. Yum!

EASY PEASY TAPIOCA PUDDING

Tapioca is gluten-free, so this is the perfect dessert to make for people who have gluten allergies.

Yield: 8 servings   *Prep time:* 5 minutes   *Cooking time:* 6 hours

2 large eggs, lightly beaten
½ cup small pearl tapioca
4 cups milk (nonfat works fine)
⅔ cup granulated sugar

Coat the inside of your slow cooker with cooking spray. In a large bowl, stir all the ingredients together. Pour the mixture into your slow cooker. Cover and cook on low for 6 hours, stirring occasionally.

TRADITIONAL FLAN

It's remarkably easy to make flan in a slow cooker. Just grab some ramekins—you should be able to fit four of them into a standard-size (6-quart) slow cooker—and get ready to impress.

Yield: 4 servings   *Prep time:* 25 minutes   *Cooking time:* 4 hours

1¼ cups granulated sugar, divided
3 large eggs
½ (14-ounce) can sweetened condensed milk
1½ cups whole milk
½ teaspoon vanilla extract

Warm a small saucepan on the stovetop over medium heat and then pour in 1 cup sugar. Stir constantly until the sugar melts and browns. Remove from the heat and spoon 3 tablespoons liquid caramel into each of 4 ramekins. Gently rotate the ramekins until the caramel coats the sides. Set aside.

In a large bowl, whisk the eggs. Add the condensed and whole milk, the remaining ¼ cup sugar, and the vanilla, whisking to mix thoroughly. To produce an extra-smooth flan, strain the mixture through cheesecloth or a fine-mesh wire strainer. Pour over the caramel in the ramekins.

Set the ramekins in the slow cooker. Carefully pour in hot water to surround them, but not enough that any will get into the ramekins. Cover and cook on high for 4 hours. Carefully lift out the flans and let them cool on trivets or a wire rack, then refrigerate for at least 1 hour.

To serve, run a knife around the edge of each ramekin and flip the chilled flans upside down onto individual serving plates.

PUMPKIN PUDDING

This spiced pumpkin pudding makes a wonderful treat on chilly autumn evenings—or any time at all. The sweet sauce, made separately, is flavored with nutmeg.

Yield: 8 servings   *Prep time:* 15 minutes   *Cooking time:* 5 hours

Pudding
½ cup unsalted butter, softened
1 cup packed brown sugar
2 large eggs
¼ cup buttermilk
1 cup pumpkin purée
1¾ cups all-purpose flour
1 teaspoon ground cinnamon
1 teaspoon ground ginger
¼ teaspoon ground cloves
1 teaspoon baking powder
1 teaspoon baking soda
½ cup chopped dates
½ cup chopped English walnuts

Whipped Cream Sauce
1 large egg
3 tablespoons unsalted butter, melted
¾ cup powdered sugar
½ teaspoon vanilla extract
¼ teaspoon ground nutmeg
½ cup heavy cream, whipped

Using an electric mixer, cream together the butter and brown sugar. Add the eggs and beat until light and fluffy.

In a separate bowl, combine the buttermilk and pumpkin. In another bowl, mix together the flour, cinnamon, ginger, cloves, baking powder, and baking soda. Add to the creamed mixture alternately with the buttermilk and pumpkin. Fold in the dates and walnuts.

Set a trivet in your slow cooker. Coat the inside of a 6-cup heatproof pudding mold with cooking spray. Pour in the pudding, set it on the trivet in the slow cooker, and cover with foil. Carefully pour in 1 inch of water around the dish.

Cover and cook on high for 5 hours.

While the pudding is cooking, make the whipped cream sauce: Beat the egg until it forms soft peaks. Mix in the melted butter, powdered sugar, vanilla, and nutmeg. Gently mix in the whipped cream.

Once the pudding has cooked, let cool, then lift out the pudding and invert onto a serving plate while still warm and serve with the sauce.

RASPBERRY CHOCOLATE CASSEROLE

Easy and delicious, this dessert casserole is likely to become a family favorite. Blueberries would also work well in this recipe—I'd use unsweetened bread for that. Garnish with whipped cream for a special dessert.

Yield: 6 servings   *Prep time:* 15 minutes   *Cooking time:* 1¾ to 2 hours

6 cups cubed brioche, challah, or Hawaiian bread
1½ cups semisweet chocolate chips
1 cup fresh raspberries
½ cup heavy cream
4 large eggs
¼ cup granulated sugar
1 teaspoon vanilla extract

Grease or spray the inside of your slow cooker. Pour in half the bread cubes, then half the chocolate chips and half the raspberries. Cover with the rest of the bread cubes and top with the remaining chocolate chips and raspberries.

In a bowl, whisk together the cream, eggs, sugar, and vanilla until well mixed. Pour over the bread mixture in the slow cooker.

Cover and cook on high for 1¾ to 2 hours, or until set. Let stand for 5 to 10 minutes before serving.

CREAMY RICE PUDDING

Rich and creamy, rice pudding comforts us and makes us smile. It's one of my very favorites!

Yield: 6 servings   *Prep time:* 5 minutes   *Cooking time:* 2 to 2½ hours

¼ cup uncooked basmati rice
2 large eggs
⅓ cup granulated sugar
1½ cups nonfat milk
1 teaspoon vanilla extract
¼ teaspoon salt
⅓ cup dried currants
ground nutmeg or cinnamon

Cook the rice according to the package directions. In a bowl, beat together the eggs, sugar, milk, vanilla, and salt. Stir in the cooked rice and the currants.

Set a trivet in your slow cooker. Place a dish that fits into your slow cooker (about 1-quart size) and pour in the pudding mixture. Sprinkle with either nutmeg or cinnamon. Cover with foil and set on the trivet in the slow cooker. Carefully pour 2 cups hot water around the dish.

Cover the slow cooker and cook on low for 2 to 2½ hours, or until the pudding is set. This dessert is delicious served either warm or cold.

LEMON RICE PUDDING WITH CARDAMOM

This dessert offers a surprising complexity of flavors. It's great topped with whipped cream.

Yield: 6 servings   *Prep time:* 15 minutes   *Cooking time:* 2 hours

4 large eggs, beaten

1 cup heavy cream

3 cups whole milk

½ cup packed light brown sugar

½ cup granulated sugar

1 teaspoon vanilla extract

2 teaspoons finely grated lemon peel

¼ teaspoon freshly grated nutmeg

5 whole green cardamom pods

3 cups cooked white rice

In your slow cooker, mix together the eggs, cream, milk, sugars, vanilla, lemon peel, nutmeg, and cardamom. Stir in the cooked rice. Cover and cook on high for 1 hour, stirring occasionally. Reduce the heat to low and cook, stirring occasionally, for 1 more hour. Remove cardamom pods. Serve the pudding either warm or cool. Garnish with candied lemon or top with whipped cream.

RICE PUDDING WITH COCONUT

Coconut adds an extra-special taste to this rice pudding. The raisins are optional, technically, but who wants rice pudding without raisins?

Yield: 6 servings   *Prep time:* 5 minutes   *Cooking time:* 4 hours

1 (12-ounce) can evaporated milk
1 (15-ounce) can sweetened cream of coconut
3 large egg yolks, lightly beaten
½ cup golden raisins (optional)
grated peel of 2 limes
1 teaspoon vanilla extract
3 cups cooked rice (basmati works well)
toasted sweetened coconut flakes, for garnish

Coat the inside of your slow cooker with cooking spray. In the slow cooker, stir together the evaporated milk, cream of coconut, egg yolks, raisins (if using), lime peel, and vanilla; mix well. Add the rice, stirring to combine.

Cover and cook on low for 4 hours, stirring occasionally. Let cool completely. The pudding will thicken as it cools. Divide into individual dishes and garnish with toasted coconut. Serve at room temperature or chilled.

OLD-FASHIONED BREAD PUDDING

This traditional-style bread pudding is easy and tasty. It stays moist by being cooked in a CorningWare or other baking dish surrounded by water.

Yield: 4 servings   *Prep time:* 15 minutes   *Cooking time:* 2½ hours

2 cups bread cubes (I like to use French bread)

⅓ cup granulated sugar

½ teaspoon ground cinnamon

½ cup raisins (optional)

2 cups whole milk

5 eggs, lightly beaten

1 teaspoon vanilla extract

¼ teaspoon salt

Use cooking spray to coat the inside of a CorningWare or other baking dish that fits inside your slow cooker. Toss the bread cubes with the sugar and cinnamon in the baking dish. If you are using the raisins, add them now.

In a separate bowl, whisk together the milk, beaten eggs, vanilla, and salt. Pour over the bread cubes in the baking dish. Set the dish in the slow cooker. Carefully pour in hot water around the dish until it comes about halfway up the side. Cover and cook on low for 2½ hours, or until a tester inserted near the center comes out clean. Let cool, covered, for 15 minutes. Serve warm.

RICH BREAD PUDDING WITH CANDIED CHERRIES

What a holiday treat! The candied cherries in this bread pudding are so Christmassy. Serve the pudding with whipped cream, and if you're feeling particular festive, stir in a few drops of red food coloring.

Yield: 5 servings   *Prep time:* 10 minutes   *Cooking time:* 4 hours

½ cup whole candied cherries

3½ cups whole milk

3 cups bread cubes (use plain white bread)

¾ cup packed light brown sugar

½ teaspoon salt

1 teaspoon ground cinnamon

2 teaspoons vanilla extract

3 large eggs, well beaten

In a large bowl, gently combine all the ingredients until the bread cubes are completely saturated.

Coat the inside of the slow cooker with cooking spray and pour in the pudding mixture.

Cover and cook on low for 4 hours, or until a tester inserted near the center comes out clean. While it's still warm, scoop into individual dishes to serve.

CINNAMON ORANGE BREAD PUDDING

It may sound crazy, but I like to eat this particular dessert for breakfast. The cinnamon and orange make such a sunny flavor combination. Serve it with an orange sauce (page 62).

Yield: 4 servings   *Prep time:* 15 minutes   *Cooking time:* 2½ hours

6 slices of French bread
1 (12-ounce) can evaporated milk
4 large eggs
2 tablespoons unsalted butter, melted
6 ounces orange juice concentrate
1 cup granulated sugar
1 teaspoon ground cinnamon
1 tablespoon vanilla extract
½ cup golden raisins

Grease with butter or spray with cooking spray a casserole dish that fits inside your slow cooker. Tear the bread into small pieces and place in the prepared dish.

In a bowl, whisk together the evaporated milk, eggs, melted butter, orange juice concentrate, sugar, cinnamon, vanilla, and raisins. Pour over the bread in the baking dish, stirring to blend well.

Tear off a 16-inch piece of foil and fold it lengthwise to form "handles" for lifting out the finished pudding. Fit the folded foil strip into the slow cooker, letting the ends hang out. Set the baking dish in the slow cooker on top of the foil.

Cover and cook on low for 2½ hours. Let cool slightly, uncovered, before serving.

SWEET POTATO BREAD PUDDING

Sweet potatoes add an interesting texture and flavor to this bread pudding, which starts with biscuits baked in the oven. An orange-flavored sauce is the finishing touch.

Yield: 7 servings   *Prep time:* 40 minutes   *Cooking time:* 4 to 5 hours

Bread Pudding
3¾ cups plus 2 tablespoons unbleached all-purpose flour
2 tablespoons baking powder
2 teaspoons salt
⅔ cup vegetable shortening
2½ plus ⅓ cup milk, divided
½ cup golden raisins
1 cup chopped pecans
4 large eggs
2½ cups half and half
¼ cup (½ stick) unsalted butter, melted
1 cup granulated sugar
1 tablespoon vanilla extract
1 teaspoon ground cinnamon
½ teaspoon ground nutmeg
1½ medium sweet potatoes or yams, baked (about 2 cups)

Orange Sauce
½ cup (1 stick) unsalted butter, softened
1 cup powdered sugar
1 teaspoon cornstarch
¼ cup orange juice
2 large egg yolks, well beaten

Preheat the oven to 450°F. In a large bowl, make a biscuit mixture by sifting the flour with the baking powder and salt, then cutting in the shortening until the mixture is nice and crumbly. Mix in 1⅓ cups milk to form a soft dough.

On a lightly floured surface, knead the dough 10 times. Drop generous spoonfuls onto a greased cookie sheet and bake for 8 to 10 minutes.

Grease your slow cooker well. Break each biscuit into 4 or 5 pieces and place in the bottom of the slow cooker. Add the raisins and pecans.

Using an electric mixer on low speed, beat the remaining 2½ cups milk with the next 7 ingredients (eggs through nutmeg). Beat the sweet potato flesh into the milk mixture, combining well. Pour over the biscuit pieces in the slow cooker. Cover and cook on low for 4 to 5 hours.

Mix the sauce ingredients together in a medium saucepan. Cook over medium heat, stirring constantly with a wire whisk for about 5 minutes, until thickened. Pour over the warm pudding on individual serving plates.

KAHLÚA BREAD PUDDING

Deliciously infused with coffee liqueur, this is a warm bread pudding with a subtle boost.

Yield: 6 to 8 servings   *Prep time:* 20 minutes   *Cooking time:* 2 to 2½ hours

½ loaf unsliced French bread, crust removed
2 (12-ounce) cans fat-free evaporated milk
3 large eggs
¼ cup Kahlúa liqueur
⅓ cup granulated sugar
¼ teaspoon ground cinnamon
1 tablespoon ground coffee
toasted sliced almonds, for garnish

Place a trivet in the bottom of the slow cooker. Grease or spray a baking dish that fits into your slow cooker.

Cut the bread into 1-inch cubes, place in a bowl, and set aside. In a blender or food processor, combine the evaporated milk, eggs, Kahlúa, sugar, cinnamon, and coffee. Blend well. Pour over the bread cubes and stir to thoroughly coat the cubes.

Pour the mixture into the prepared dish and set it on the trivet in your slow cooker. Cover the dish with foil. Carefully pour 2 cups of hot water into the slow cooker around the pudding dish.

Cover the slow cooker and cook on high for 2 to 2½ hours, or until a knife inserted near the center comes out clean. Sprinkle with toasted almonds before serving. Serve warm.

INDIAN PUDDING

You've probably heard of hasty pudding. Well, Indian pudding is hasty pudding with extra oomph. The addition of cinnamon and ginger makes this sweet treat hard to resist.

Yield: 4 servings   *Prep time:* 20 minutes   *Cooking time:* 6 to 8 hours

3 cups milk

½ cup cornmeal

3 large eggs

½ teaspoon salt

¼ cup packed light brown sugar

⅓ cup light molasses

½ teaspoon ground cinnamon

½ teaspoon ground ginger

¼ teaspoon ground allspice

2 tablespoons unsalted butter, melted

Lightly grease the inside of your slow cooker or spray with cooking spray. Preheat the cooker on high for 20 minutes.

In a medium saucepan over medium heat, bring the milk and cornmeal to a boil. Let boil for 5 minutes, reduce heat and cover, and continue to cook for 10 more minutes.

In a separate bowl, whisk the eggs with all the remaining ingredients. Gradually beat in the cornmeal mixture; whisk until smooth. Pour the pudding mixture into the slow cooker. Cover and cook on low for 6 to 8 hours. Serve warm.

CHAPTER 4

COOKIES, BROWNIES, AND BARS

COCOA BROWNIES

Cooking brownies from scratch is a snap. Just stir together the ingredients and let your slow cooker do the rest.

Yield: 12 brownies   *Prep time:* 10 minutes   *Cooking time:* 2 to 3 hours

⅔ cup granulated sugar

⅔ cup unbleached all-purpose flour

1 teaspoon baking powder

⅓ cup unsweetened cocoa powder

¼ teaspoon salt

⅔ cup reduced-fat evaporated milk

1 large egg, well-beaten

⅓ cup unsalted butter, melted

1½ teaspoons vanilla extract

1 cup semisweet chocolate chips

Coat the inside of a 4-quart slow cooker with cooking spray. In a bowl, stir together the dry ingredients (sugar through salt) to combine thoroughly.

In another bowl, mix together the evaporated milk, egg, melted butter, and vanilla. Stir into the dry ingredients, but don't overmix. Stir in the chocolate chips.

Transfer the dough to the slow cooker, smoothing the top. Cover and cook on low for 2 to 3 hours, or until a toothpick inserted near the center comes out clean. Let cool with the lid off for about 15 minutes and then either turn out onto a serving plate, or cut into squares right in the slow cooker.

TRIPLE CHOCOLATE BROWNIES

Moist and intensely chocolatey, these brownies are for the hard-core chocoholic!

Yield: 10 servings   *Prep time:* 20 minutes   *Cooking time:* 4 hours

1¼ cups unbleached all-purpose flour

¼ cup unsweetened cocoa powder

¾ teaspoon baking powder

½ teaspoon sea salt

½ cup (1 stick) unsalted butter, cut into pieces

8 ounces bittersweet chocolate, chopped into small pieces

1 cup granulated sugar

3 large eggs, well beaten

1 cup chopped walnuts (optional)

1 cup semisweet chocolate chips (I like Ghirardelli)

Coat the inside of your slow cooker with cooking spray. Cover the bottom with parchment paper and spray the paper.

In a bowl, whisk together the flour, cocoa, baking powder, and salt. In another bowl, microwave the butter and chopped chocolate together on high, checking it every 30 seconds just until the chocolate is melted—you don't want to burn it. Alternatively, you can use a double boiler to melt the chocolate and butter over the stovetop. Stir in the sugar and then whisk in the eggs, mixing well.

Combine the flour and chocolate mixtures, then stir in the walnuts, if using; and chocolate chips; don't overmix. Spread in your slow cooker and smooth the top.

Cover and cook on low for 3½ hours. Remove the slow cooker lid and cook another 30 minutes. Run a knife around the outside edge and let the brownies cool completely after you've taken the ceramic liner out and placed on a rack to cool. Turn the brownies out onto a serving plate and cut into squares.

COCONUT BROWNIE BARS

You probably won't be able to eat just one of these rich brownies. Take them to your next work function or other get-together and be the hero!

Yield: 12 brownies   *Prep time:* 20 minutes   *Cooking time:* 4 hours

1 cup granulated sugar

½ cup (1 stick) unsalted butter, melted

1 teaspoon vanilla extract

2 large eggs

⅓ cup unsweetened cocoa powder

¼ teaspoon salt

¼ teaspoon baking powder

1 cup sweetened flaked coconut, divided

Coat the inside of your slow cooker with cooking spray. In a small bowl, stir together the sugar, butter, and vanilla. Add the eggs, mixing well with a spoon.

In a separate small bowl, mix together the cocoa, salt, and baking powder; add in small batches to the wet ingredients. Stir in ¾ cup of the coconut. Spread in the bottom of your slow cooker and sprinkle the remaining ¼ cup coconut on top.

Cover and cook on low for 4 hours, until a sharp knife inserted near the center comes out clean. Let cool. Cut into pieces and serve.

BANANA BREAD

Use a disposable 8-inch pan to make this banana bread, and you can give away a loaf without worrying about getting your pan back!

Yield: 6 servings (1 loaf)   *Prep time:* 20 minutes   *Cooking time:* 6 hours

½ cup (1 stick) unsalted butter, softened

2 large eggs

1 cup granulated sugar

¼ cup whole milk

1 teaspoon vanilla extract

1 cup mashed bananas (about 2 medium)

2 cups unbleached all-purpose flour

1 teaspoon baking soda

½ teaspoon salt

½ cup chopped walnuts (optional)

Using an electric mixer, blend together the butter, eggs, sugar, milk, and vanilla. Add the mashed bananas.

In a separate bowl, combine the flour, baking soda, and salt; add to the banana mixture. Add the nuts, if you are using them. Don't overmix the batter.

Coat the inside of an 8-inch bread pan with cooking spray. Pour in the bread mixture and set the pan in your slow cooker. Cover and cook on low for 6 hours, until a toothpick inserted near the center comes out clean.

Let cool before removing from the slow cooker. Remove and cool completely on a rack.

LEMON BARS

Lemon makes a welcome taste change for the dessert table. These are sure to please!

Yield: 14 bars   *Prep time:* 25 minutes   *Cooking time:* 4 hours

1 cup plus 2 tablespoons unbleached all-purpose flour, divided

½ teaspoon baking powder

¼ cup powdered sugar

½ cup (1 stick) unsalted butter

2 large eggs

1 cup granulated sugar

2 tablespoons lemon juice

1 tablespoon grated lemon peel

Grease or spray the inside of your slow cooker. For the bottom layer of the bars, combine 1 cup flour with the baking powder, powdered sugar, and butter. Beat with electric mixer until the mixture can hold a shape. Press into the bottom of the slow cooker.

Using an electric mixer, beat the eggs, granulated sugar, lemon juice, lemon peel, and remaining 2 tablespoons flour. Pour the lemon mixture over the dough layer in the slow cooker.

Cover and cook on low for 4 hours. Let cool completely before cutting into bars.

MACAROON BROWNIE BARS

Many countries have their own version of the macaroon, traditionally a light little cake made with ground almonds. These scrumptious brownies evoke the taste and texture of a macaroon.

Yield: 18 bars   *Prep time:* 25 minutes   *Cooking time:* 6 hours

1 cup (2 sticks) unsalted butter, softened
2 cups granulated sugar
4 large eggs
2½ teaspoons vanilla extract, divided
2 cups unbleached all-purpose flour
¾ teaspoon cream of tartar
½ cup unsweetened cocoa powder
½ cup chopped toasted almonds
4 cups unsweetened shredded sweetened coconut
1 (14-ounce) can sweetened condensed milk

Coat the inside of the slow cooker with cooking spray. Using an electric mixer, cream the butter and sugar. Add the eggs, and then 1½ teaspoons vanilla.

In a separate bowl, combine the flour, cream of tartar, and cocoa. Add to the creamed mixture and then stir in the almonds and spread half of this batter in the bottom of your slow cooker.

In a large bowl, mix the coconut, condensed milk, and remaining teaspoon of vanilla extract. Spread the coconut mixture over the batter in the slow cooker. Top with the rest of the batter.

Cover and cook on low for 6 hours, or until done (until a toothpick inserted near the center comes out clean). Let cool and cut into squares to serve either warm or cold—these bars are good either way.

CHOCOLATE CHIP COOKIE BARS

Traditional cookies and slow cookers may be a no-go, but these bars are a great twist on standard chocolate chip cookies. Make them for PTA meetings, parties, and any other event where you want to wow the guests.

Yield: 6 to 8 servings   *Prep time:* 15 minutes   *Cooking time:* 4 hours

1 cup (2 sticks) unsalted butter

¾ cup granulated sugar

¾ cup packed light brown sugar

2 large eggs

½ teaspoon vanilla extract

1¾ cups unbleached all-purpose flour

1 teaspoon baking soda

⅓ cup creamy peanut butter

1 cup semisweet chocolate chips

½ cup milk chocolate chips

Using an electric mixer, cream the butter together with both types of sugar. Add the eggs and mix well. Add the vanilla.

In another bowl, combine the flour and baking soda. Using a wooden spoon, stir the dry ingredients into the creamed mixture. When everything is fully combined, add the peanut butter and chocolate chips.

Coat the inside of the slow cooker with cooking spray. Spread the cookie mixture in the bottom of the cooker. Cover and cook on low for 4 hours. Let cool, then cut into bars for serving.

CHOCOLATE CHIP PEANUT BUTTER BARS

Who needs store-bought sweets when these chocolatey, peanutty bars are so easy to make? These are truly yummy!

Yield: 10 bars   *Prep time:* 15 minutes   *Cooking time:* 2½ hours

1 cup creamy peanut butter

5 tablespoons unsalted butter, softened

½ cup granulated sugar

2 large eggs

1 teaspoon vanilla extract

2 cups unbleached all-purpose flour

¼ teaspoon baking powder

1 cup milk chocolate chips

Coat the inside of your slow cooker with cooking spray. In a large bowl, combine the peanut butter, butter, sugar, eggs, and vanilla. Add the flour and baking powder, mixing well. Stir in the chocolate chips. Spread the dough into the bottom of the slow cooker.

Cover the slow cooker but leave the lid tilted a bit to release steam. Cook on high for about 2½ hours, or until a toothpick inserted near the center comes out clean. Cool in the cooker and then invert onto a plate. Cut into bars.

BLONDIES

This recipe is perfect for those of you who don't love chocolate but do love chewy, delicious goodness. This will become one of your favorites!

Yield: 10 bars   *Prep time:* 10 minutes   *Cooking time:* 6 to 8 hours

⅓ cup unsalted butter, softened

1 cup packed light brown sugar

1 large egg

1 teaspoon vanilla extract

1 cup unbleached all-purpose flour

½ teaspoon baking powder

⅛ teaspoon baking soda

½ teaspoon salt

½ cup chopped walnuts

⅔ cup semisweet chocolate chips

⅔ cup caramel or butterscotch chips

Grease the inside of your slow cooker, or coat with cooking spray. Using an electric mixer, cream together the butter and brown sugar; beat in the egg and vanilla. Add the flour, baking powder, baking soda, and salt. Stir in the walnuts and chips.

Spread the cookie dough into the bottom of your slow cooker. Cover and cook on low for 6 to 8 hours, or until set. Let cool and cut into squares.

LUSCIOUS STRAWBERRY BROWNIES

The addition of strawberries gives a new flavor profile to the traditional brownie. Sure to be a hit with both kids and adults, these are especially good served with more sliced strawberries and whipped cream.

Yield: 12 to 15 brownies   *Prep time:* 10 minutes   *Cooking time:* 6 to 7 hours

1 cup (2 sticks) unsalted butter, melted and cooled
1 large egg
1 tablespoon vanilla extract
2 cups strawberries, sliced, divided
1½ cups cake flour, or as needed
1 cup granulated sugar
½ cup unsweetened cocoa powder

Coat the inside of your slow cooker with cooking spray. In a large bowl, whisk together the butter, egg, and vanilla.

Whirl about ¼ cup strawberries in a blender or food processor. Stir into the butter mixture, combining well.

Stir together the cake flour, sugar, and cocoa. Combine with the butter mixture. Gently fold in the rest of the strawberries. The batter will be thinner than typical cookie dough, but you don't want it to be too runny. If it seems too wet, add about ¼ cup more cake flour. Pour into the slow cooker.

Cover and cook on low for 6 to 7 hours, or until a toothpick inserted near the center comes out clean. Invert immediately onto a wire rack to cool.

SHORTBREAD

These tender little shortbread cookies are excellent served alongside your favorite fruit compote or spread with your favorite jelly.

Yield: 24 to 36 cookies   *Prep time:* 25 minutes   *Cooking time:* 2 to 3 hours

3 cups unbleached all-purpose flour
1 cup ultrafine granulated sugar (baker's sugar)
1 cup (2 sticks) unsalted butter
2 tablespoons coarse sugar

Using an electric mixer, cream together the butter and sugar. Add 2½ cups of the flour and mix well. On a work surface floured with the remaining ½ cup flour, knead the shortbread dough to incorporate the flour.

Coat the inside of the slow cooker with cooking spray. Press the shortbread mixture into the bottom of the cooker and score the dough to mark square portions. Sprinkle with the coarse sugar.

Cover and cook on low for 2 to 3 hours. Let cool, then cut the shortbread into the scored squares

CHAPTER 5

FRUIT COMPOTES, SPREADS, AND SAUCES

WARM AND GOOEY FRUIT COMPOTE

This makes a great topping for ice cream, pound cake, or even oatmeal for breakfast!

Yield: 15 servings   *Prep time:* 15 minutes   *Cooking time:* 5 to 6 hours

1 (8.5 ounce) can pineapple chunks, drained

1 (8.5 ounce) can pears halves, drained

1 (8.5 ounce) can peaches slices, drained

1 (8.5 ounce) can cherry pie filling

1 cup packed light brown sugar

1 teaspoon ground cinnamon

½ cup (1 stick) unsalted butter, cut into pieces

Cut all the fruit into small chunks and place in a 4½-quart slow cooker. Stir in the sugar and cinnamon and dot the whole mixture with the butter pieces. Cover and cook on low for 5 to 6 hours. Serve warm.

SPICED FRUIT MEDLEY

Here's a fruit dessert that has a little punch, thanks to its sweet spices. It's especially good served with vanilla ice cream.

Yield: 8 servings   *Prep time:* 10 minutes   *Cooking time:* 4 to 6 hours

¾ cup maraschino cherries, drained

1 (28-ounce) can pear slices, drained

16 ounces canned pineapple tidbits, including juice

1 (28-ounce) can peach slices, drained

1 (15-ounce) can mixed fruit

¼ cup (½ stick) unsalted butter

1 tablespoon cornstarch

½ cup packed dark brown sugar

1 teaspoon ground nutmeg

1½ teaspoons ground cinnamon

½ teaspoon ground cloves

Place all the ingredients in a 4½-quart slow cooker. Stir gently to mix, but don't break up the fruit pieces. Cover and cook on low for 4 to 6 hours. Serve warm.

APPLE CRANBERRY COMPOTE

This just speaks of cool fall air, football season, and colorful leaves on the trees. Comfort food, anyone?

Yield: 4 to 6 servings   *Prep time:* 10 minutes   *Cooking time:* 4 to 6 hours

6 Granny Smith apples, peeled, cored, and sliced
1 cup cranberries (fresh are best)
1 cup granulated sugar
½ teaspoon grated orange peel
½ cup water
3 tablespoons orange juice
heavy cream, for serving

Arrange the apple slices in the bottom of the slow cooker and sprinkle the cranberries on top of them. In a small bowl, combine the sugar and the orange peel; sprinkle over the fruit in the slow cooker. Mix the orange juice and water together and pour it in, lightly stirring to combine.

Cover and cook on low for 4 to 6 hours, until the apples are tender. Serve in dessert bowls and pass around cream to pour over the compotes.

SIMMERED SWEET PLUMS

This makes a fine dessert topped with just a bit of fresh cream, ice cream, or plain or vanilla Greek yogurt. But don't limit these plums to the end of the meal—they also make an excellent garnish for roast pork tenderloin.

Yield: 20 servings   *Prep time:* 30 minutes   *Cooking time:* 3 hours

3 pounds fresh, ripe plums (about 14 standard-size plums)

1 teaspoon ground cinnamon

¾ cup granulated sugar (more if the plums aren't especially sweet)

¼ cup cold purified water

2 tablespoons cornstarch

Pit the plums and cut them into quarters. Toss the plum pieces with the cinnamon and sugar right in the slow cooker.

In a glass measuring cup, stir together the water and cornstarch until totally combined. Pour over the plums to thicken the juices as the fruit cooks. Cover and cook on low for 3 hours. Serve warm.

FUNKY, CHUNKY APPLESAUCE

Everybody loves applesauce, and this is so much better than what comes out of a can or jar. I prefer Granny Smith apples for their firm texture and tart flavor.

Yield: 10 servings   *Prep time:* 15 minutes   *Cooking time:* 10 to 11 hours

½ cup purified water

1 cup granulated sugar

2 tablespoons packed light brown sugar

¾ teaspoon ground cloves

11 large Granny Smith apples, peeled, cored, and cut into chunks

Combine all the ingredients in a 4½-quart slow cooker and stir well. Cover and cook on low for 10 to 11 hours, stirring occasionally.

CINNAMON FRUIT JUMBLE

For a light dessert or a sweet brunch dish, try this cinnamon-flavored fruit combo. I generally use canned fruits for the sake of convenience, but fresh fruit works well when it's in season. It all depends on how much time you have and what you have on hand in your kitchen.

Yield: 10 servings   *Prep time:* 10 minutes   *Cooking time:* 3 to 5 hours

1 (15-ounce) can sweet dark cherries, drained

1 (15-ounce) can apricot halves, drained

1 (15-ounce) can sliced peaches, drained

1 (15-ounce) can sliced pears, drained

¼ cup freshly squeezed orange juice

¾ teaspoon ground cinnamon

¼ cup packed light brown sugar

Mix all the drained fruits together in a 4½-quart slow cooker. Stir in the orange juice, cinnamon, and brown sugar, mixing well. Cover and cook on low for 3 to 5 hours. Serve warm.

EASY APPLE BUTTER

You can use either homemade or jarred applesauce for this. Use it as a topping for biscuits, toast, dessert bread, and more. Seal it in pretty jars to give as holiday or hostess gifts.

Yield: 28 servings or more   *Prep time:* 10 minutes   *Cooking time:* 15 hours

7 cups applesauce
1 cup apple cider
1 teaspoon ground cinnamon
¼ teaspoon ground cloves
½ teaspoon ground allspice
1½ cups honey

Combine all the ingredients in a 4½-quart slow cooker. Cover and cook on low for 15 hours (or longer), stirring occasionally, until the apple butter turns a deep brown color.

If you won't be using all the apple butter at one go, spoon it into sterilized jars and seal with sterile lids.

TROPICAL-STYLE BANANAS

This one will put you in mind of balmy nights and warm tropical breezes!

Yield: 8 servings   *Prep time:* 5 minutes   *Cooking time:* 2 hours

6 firm but ripe bananas
½ teaspoon ground cinnamon
¼ teaspoon salt
½ cup sweetened flaked coconut
½ cup dark corn syrup
¼ cup (½ stick) unsalted butter, melted
1 tablespoon grated lemon peel
3 to 4 tablespoons lemon juice

Place the bananas in the bottom of the slow cooker. Sprinkle with the cinnamon, salt, and coconut.

In a small bowl, mix together the corn syrup, butter, lemon peel, and lemon juice to taste. Pour over the bananas. Cover and cook on low for 2 hours. Serve warm, spooning sauce over it.

CREAMY PEACHES

This peach dish is a nice finish to a comforting home-cooked meal, or it makes a welcome bring-along for potluck gatherings.

Yield: 8 to 10 servings   *Prep time:* 10 minutes   *Cooking time:* 6 to 8 hours

½ cup packed light brown sugar
½ cup granulated sugar
¾ cup Bisquick baking mix
2 eggs
2 teaspoons unsalted butter, melted
2 teaspoons vanilla extract
3 tablespoons heavy cream
2 cups mashed fresh peaches
1 teaspoon ground cinnamon

Combine the sugars and Bisquick in a bowl. In a separate bowl, whisk together the eggs, butter, vanilla, and cream. Combine with the dry ingredients.

Coat the inside of your slow cooker with cooking spray. Scoop the mashed peaches into the cooker; sprinkle with cinnamon.

Spoon the Bisquick batter over the peaches. Cover and cook on low for 6 to 8 hours. Serve warm.

DRIED PLUM DELIGHT

Greatly underrated, prunes cook to such a tender sweetness that you hardly know you're eating something so good for you!

Yield: 6 to 8 servings   *Prep time:* 10 minutes   *Cooking time:* 3 hours

2 cups pitted dried prunes

peel from half an orange or lemon, removed in strips using a peeler

1 cup granulated sugar, divided

⅔ cup boiling water

½ cup chopped walnuts (optional)

sweetened whipped cream, for serving

Soak the prunes overnight in enough water to cover. Drain and place the soaked prunes in the bottom of your slow cooker. Sprinkle the strips of peel on top of the prunes. Add ½ cup sugar, then pour in the ⅔ cup boiling water. Add the remaining ½ cup sugar and nuts, if desired.

Cover and cook on high for 3 hours. Discard the strips of peel. Spoon the prunes into serving dishes and top with whipped cream. Serve warm.

CHAPTER 6

EMERGENCY DESSERTS

LUSH PLUMPED FRUIT

The slow cooking process plumps the dried fruit, bringing out its natural sweetness so the flavors simply explode on the tongue. Plain Greek yogurt, vanilla ice cream, or whipped cream makes a delicious finishing touch.

Yield: 12 servings   *Prep time:* 5 minutes   *Cooking time:* 8 hours

8 ounces dried pears

8 ounces dried apricots

1 pound pitted dried prunes

3 cups purified water

½ cup granulated sugar

½ teaspoon vanilla extract

1 teaspoon finely grated lemon peel

2 tablespoons freshly squeezed lemon juice

Combine all the ingredients in your slow cooker and cook on low for 8 hours, until the fruit is tender. Spoon into individual dessert dishes to serve either warmed or chilled.

BROWNIE PUDDING CAKE

This chocolatey pudding is so good that it's likely to become a true family favorite. Serve it with whipped cream or ice cream—delicious!

Yield: 8 servings   *Prep time:* 10 minutes   *Cooking time:* 5 hours

1 (4-serving) package instant chocolate pudding mix

1 box chocolate cake mix

4 large eggs

1 pint sour cream

¾ cup canola oil

1 cup water

1 cup semisweet chocolate chips

1 cup chopped toasted pecans (optional)

Coat the inside of your slow cooker with cooking spray.

Mix all the ingredients, except chocolate chips and toasted pecans, if using, together in a large bowl. Beat, using an electric mixer, then stir in the chocolate chips and pecans, if using. Pour the batter into the slow cooker. Cover and cook on low for 5 hours. Serve warm or chilled.

GERMAN CHOCOLATE UPSIDE-DOWN CAKE

When you consider how long it can take to make a German chocolate cake, this one is such a treat! It requires very little effort, and your can walk away for several hours while it cooks. Can you think of a better way to have German chocolate cake for dessert tonight?

Yield: 10 servings   *Prep time:* 20 minutes   *Cooking time:* 5 to 5½ hours

2 tablespoons unsalted butter

½ cup water

⅔ cup packed light brown sugar

¼ cup toasted sweetened shredded coconut, divided

2 large eggs

1 cup buttermilk

½ cup light sour cream

⅓ cup applesauce

1 box German chocolate cake mix

⅓ cup chopped pecans (optional)

Coat the inside of your slow cooker with cooking spray. Turn the slow cooker on high.

In a small saucepan over medium-high heat, melt the butter with the water. Stir in the brown sugar until smooth. Pour into the slow cooker and sprinkle with half of the coconut.

Using an electric mixer, beat the eggs until frothy, then beat in the buttermilk, sour cream, and applesauce. Add the cake mix and beat on low for 30 seconds to combine, then beat on high for 2 more minutes. Pour into the slow cooker.

Cover and cook on low for 4½ to 5 hours, then remove the lid and cook for 30 minutes longer. Turn off the slow cooker and let the cake cool in the slow cooker for 30 minutes with the lid removed. Then turn out the cake onto a serving plate and top with the remaining coconut and the pecans, if using. Let cool completely before serving. If you find you have more time, make the topping recipe on page 21 for a more decadent cake.

SIMPLE CAKE, ANY FLAVOR

This one is totally up to you, if you're in a chocolate mood, make the cake chocolate. If you feel more like lemon, make it a lemon cake. The choices are practically endless!

Yield: 8 servings   *Prep time:* 5 minutes   *Cooking time:* 6 hours

1 box cake mix, any flavor you choose

1 (4-serving) package instant pudding, the same flavor as
    your cake mix

4 large eggs

1½ cups reduced-fat sour cream

1 cup water

¾ cup canola oil

Coat the inside of your slow cooker with cooking spray. Using an electric mixer, combine all of the ingredients to make a smooth batter. Pour into the slow cooker.

Cover and cook on low for 6 hours. Turn off the slow cooker and let the cake sit for a couple more hours, covered. Then turn it out onto a plate to serve either warm or cooled.

LEMON CAKE

Pleasantly tart, this cake is a treat for brunch or any time you want something light and tasty.

Yield: 8 servings   *Prep time:* 20 minutes   *Cooking time:* 2 to 2½ hours

1 box lemon-poppyseed bread mix
1 cup sour cream
1 large egg
1¼ cups water, divided
½ cup granulated sugar
1 tablespoon unsalted butter
¼ cup lemon juice

In a large bowl, stir the bread mix together with the sour cream, egg, and ½ cup water until well blended. Coat the inside of your slow cooker with cooking spray and pour in the batter.

To prepare a lemon sauce to go over the batter, combine the remaining ¾ cup water, sugar, butter, and lemon juice in a medium saucepan. Bring to a boil over high heat, cook for about 7 minutes, until thickened and then pour the sauce over the batter in the slow cooker.

Cover and cook on high for 2 to 2½ hours. Turn off the heat and let cool for 30 minutes with the lid tilted so the steam can escape. When cool, invert onto a serving plate.

FRUIT PUDDING CAKE

Zwieback isn't just for teething babies. It makes a satisfyingly crunchy topping for this pudding.

Yield: 8 servings   *Prep time:* 10 minutes   *Cooking time:* 3 to 4 hours

14 slices zwieback toast, finely crushed (about 1 ½ cups)

½ cup (1 stick) unsalted butter, melted

½ cup packed light brown sugar

1 teaspoon ground cinnamon

2 cups applesauce (or 2 cups pitted fresh cherries or cut-up
    plums, pears, or apples)

In a bowl, thoroughly mix the zwieback crumbs with the melted butter, brown sugar, and cinnamon.

Spoon the applesauce (or other fruit) into a 1-quart baking dish that fits into your slow cooker. Top with the crumb mixture. Set the dish in the slow cooker.

Cover and cook on low for 3 to 4 hours. This dish tastes good either warm or cold. Just spoon it out of the slow cooker into individual serving dishes.

EASY CHOCOLATE CAKE

Top this moist chocolate cake with store-bought frosting, or serve it with ice cream.

Yield: 8 servings   *Prep time:* 15 minutes   *Cooking time:* 6 hours

1 box chocolate cake mix
1 pint sour cream
4 large eggs
1 (4-serving) package instant chocolate pudding mix
1 cup water
¾ cup canola oil

Coat the inside of your slow cooker with cooking spray.

Combine all the ingredients in a large bowl. Pour the cake batter into the slow cooker. Cover and cook on low for 6 hours. Cool for 30 minutes and then invert onto a serving plate. Frost, if desired (see frosting options on pages 7, 9, or 25).

APPLE BUTTERSCOTCH CRISP

The touch of butterscotch makes this dessert special. Top it with ice cream or whipped cream, if you wish.

Yield: 8 servings   *Prep time:* 10 minutes   *Cooking time:* 5 hours

6 cups peeled, cored, and sliced Granny Smith apples
½ cup unbleached all-purpose flour
½ cup quick-cooking rolled oats
¾ cup packed light brown sugar
1 (4-serving) package instant butterscotch pudding mix
1 teaspoon ground cinnamon
½ cup (1 stick) very cold unsalted butter

Coat the inside of your slow cooker with cooking spray. Pour the sliced apples into the slow cooker.

In a bowl, combine the flour, oats, brown sugar, pudding mix, and cinnamon. Cut in the cold butter to make a crumbly mixture. Sprinkle over the sliced apples.

Cover and cook on low for 5 hours. Spoon the crisp into dessert cups to serve warm or cooled.

EASY-DAY BLUEBERRY CAKE

This is the easiest dessert ever, with a minimum of ingredients but maximum flavor. Top it with whipped cream.

Yield: 8 servings   *Prep time:* 5 minutes   *Cooking time:* 2 to 3 hours

1 (21-ounce) can blueberry pie filling
1 box yellow cake mix
½ cup (1 stick) unsalted butter, softened
½ cup chopped walnuts

Grease or spray the inside of your slow cooker. Pour the blueberry pie filling into the slow cooker.

In a bowl, stir the cake mix together with the butter to make a crumbly mixture. Sprinkle over the blueberry pie filling in the slow cooker. The walnuts go on top of that.

Cover and cook on low for 2 to 3 hours. Serve warm.

CREAMY, DREAMY BANANA UPSIDE-DOWN CAKE

You're probably familiar with pineapple upside-down cake. That's good, but when what you're craving is a creamy, banana-flavored concoction, this is just the thing.

Yield: 8 servings   *Prep time:* 10 minutes   *Cooking time:* 2 hours

3 large egg whites
1 cup mashed bananas (about 2 medium bananas)
1 box yellow cake mix
2½ cups water, divided
1 box yellow cake mix
1 (6-serving) package banana pudding mix (not instant)

Coat the inside of your slow cooker with cooking spray. Turn the slow cooker to high.

In a bowl, beat the egg whites with your electric mixer for 2 minutes or so, until soft peaks form (2 minutes or so). Beat the mashed banana with the electric mixer in a separate bowl. Combine the bananas and egg whites. Add the cake mix and ½ cup water and beat for 2 minutes, until thick and creamy.

Pour the remaining 2 cups water into the slow cooker. Sprinkle in the pudding mix and stir until thoroughly combined. Evenly pour in the cake batter, but don't stir it. Drape a paper towel over the top of the slow cooker, cover the slow cooker, and cook on high for 2 hours.

Once the cake has finished cooking, remove the lid and paper towel and invert a serving plate over the slow cooker. Using both hands (and maybe a helper), flip the slow cooker upside down to deposit the cake on the serving plate. The cake will be hot and sauce will be dribbling out at the sides, so be extra careful. Serve warm.

STRAWBERRY CAKE

If you're a strawberry lover, here's a cake that's sure to make you happy. It would make a lovely addition to a spring dinner or even a wedding shower. Light and luscious, it will be a crowd-pleaser.

Yield: 8 servings   *Prep time:* 5 minutes   *Cooking time:* 2 to 3 hours

1 (21-ounce) can strawberry pie filling, or 1½ cups fresh
   strawberry pieces

1 box strawberry or yellow cake mix

½ cup (1 stick) unsalted butter, melted

⅓ cup chopped walnuts (optional)

1 container of whipped topping such as Cool Whip

Coat the inside of your slow cooker with cooking spray. Pour the pie filling or fresh strawberries into the slow cooker.

In a bowl, mix together the cake mix and the melted butter; it will make a crumbly mixture. Sprinkle over the strawberries in the slow cooker. Sprinkle in the walnuts, if you are using them.

Cover and cook on low for 2 to 3 hours. Cool for about 10 minutes, then scoop into serving dishes and top with the Cool Whip.

CHOCOLATE SUNDAE SURPRISE CAKE

The surprise is how good this tastes, and how easy it is to prepare.
Serve with whipped cream or ice cream to complete your "sundae."

Yield: 8 servings   *Prep time:* 10 minutes   *Cooking time:* 3 to 4 hours

1 cup unbleached all-purpose flour

½ cup granulated sugar

¼ cup unsweetened cocoa powder

2 teaspoons baking powder

½ teaspoon salt

½ cup chopped pecans

¼ cup canola oil

½ cup milk

1 teaspoon vanilla extract

1 cup boiling water

½ cup chocolate syrup

Use cooking spray to coat the inside of a 6-cup baking dish that fits into
your slow cooker.

In a mixing bowl, combine the flour, sugar, cocoa, baking powder, salt,
and pecans. Add the oil, milk, and vanilla. Pour the batter into the prepared
baking dish.

In a separate bowl, mix the boiling water and chocolate syrup. Slowly
pour the mixture over the baking dish.

Place a trivet in the slow cooker and set the baking dish on the trivet.
Drape 4 paper towels over the slow cooker and cover with the lid. Cook on
low for 3 to 4 hours. Let cool, uncovered and serve on dessert plates.

PREACHER'S DELIGHT

Here's the ideal dessert for those Sundays when you've invited your preacher to dinner after church. Turn it on before you go, and it will be done when you get home. And will the house smell great! Serve this with vanilla ice cream, if you like.

Yield: 8 servings   *Prep time:* 10 minutes   *Cooking time:* 2 to 3 hours

1 (21-ounce) can cherry pie filling
1 box yellow cake mix
½ cup (1 stick) unsalted butter, melted
⅓ cup chopped walnuts

Coat the inside of your slow cooker with cooking spray. Spoon in the cherry pie filling.

Combine the cake mix with the butter to make a crumbly mixture. Sprinkle over the pie filling in the slow cooker and top with the chopped nuts.

Cover and cook on low for 2 to 3 hours.

QUICK PECAN BROWNIES

These brownies are good either with or without the pecans.

Yield: 6 to 8 servings   *Prep time:* 15 minutes   *Cooking time:* 3 hours

1 large brownie mix (use a really good one, such as
    Ghirardelli)

ingredients called for on the brownie package (usually eggs,
    milk, and canola oil)

¼ cup (½ stick) unsalted butter, melted

1 cup chopped pecans

Mix the brownie batter according to the package directions.

Swirl the melted butter inside a 5-inch cake pan or coffee can to coat the bottom and sides. Sprinkle in half of the pecans; stir the rest into the brownie batter. Pour the batter into the container and place it in your slow cooker. Layer 8 paper towels on top of the container.

Cover and cook on high for 3 hours. Turn off the heat, but don't take off the lid or disturb the slow cooker for at least 1 hour. Then remove the container from the slow cooker, discard the paper towels, and let stand for 5 to 10 minutes.

Remove from the cake pan, invert onto a plate and serve warm, or let cool completely. Slice or cut into squares.

CONVERSIONS

MEASURE	EQUIVALENT	METRIC
1 teaspoon	—	5.0 milliliters
1 tablespoon	3 teaspoons	14.8 milliliters
1 cup	16 tablespoons	236.8 milliliters
1 pint	2 cups	473.6 milliliters
1 quart	4 cups	947.2 milliliters
1 liter	4 cups + 3½ tablespoons	1000 milliliters
1 ounce (dry)	2 tablespoons	28.35 grams
1 pound	16 ounces	453.49 grams
2.21 pounds	35.3 ounces	1 kilogram
325°F/350°F/375°F	—	165°C/177°C/190°C

RECIPE INDEX

ACKNOWLEDGMENTS

To my daughter, Elizabeth, of course, for her help and her mad editing skills. And to the strong, vibrant, wonderful women in my family, starting with my sweet mother. We miss you every day.

ABOUT THE AUTHOR

JONNIE DOWNING and her daughter, Elizabeth, run the website CrockpotNinja.com and have a great time finding and creating new recipes for the slow cooker. This collection, a variety of desserts that are a combination of new recipes and old family recipes modified for the slow cooker, was a labor of love intended to bring some sweetness into the lives of her readers. Jonnie is also author of *Holiday Slow Cooker*.